summer spy

sexy adjective

\ 'sek-sē \

sexier; sexiest

Definition of *sexy*

1: sexually suggestive or stimulating :
EROTIC

2: generally attractive or interesting :
APPEALINGa *sexy* stock

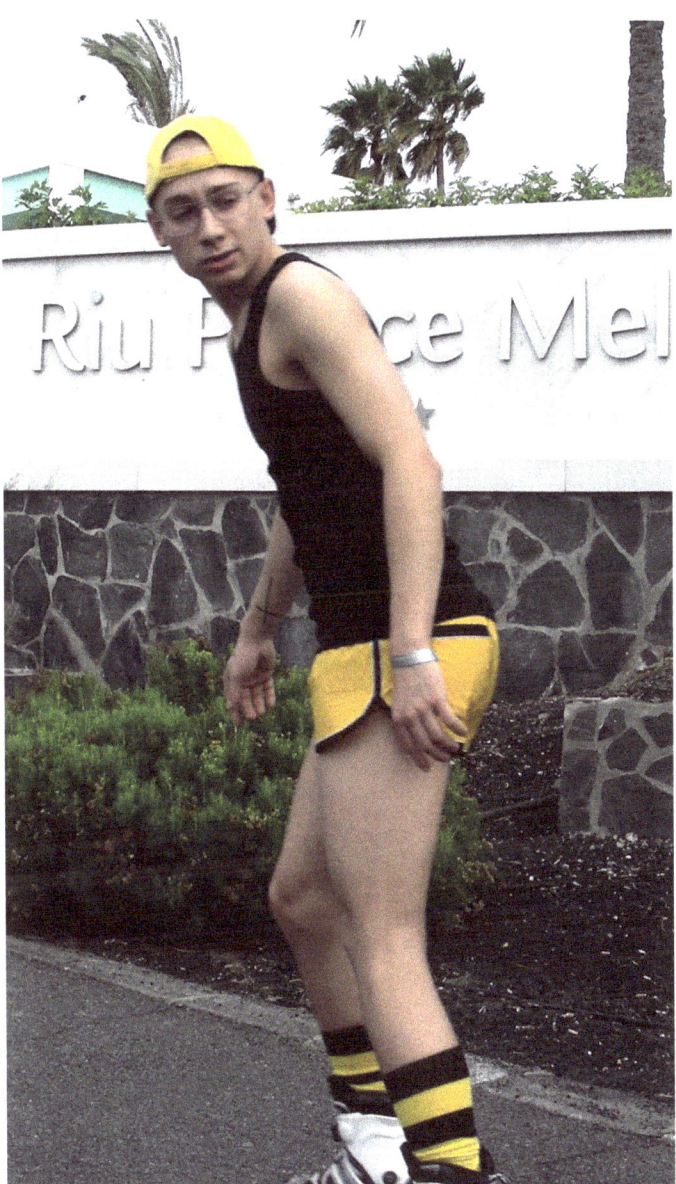

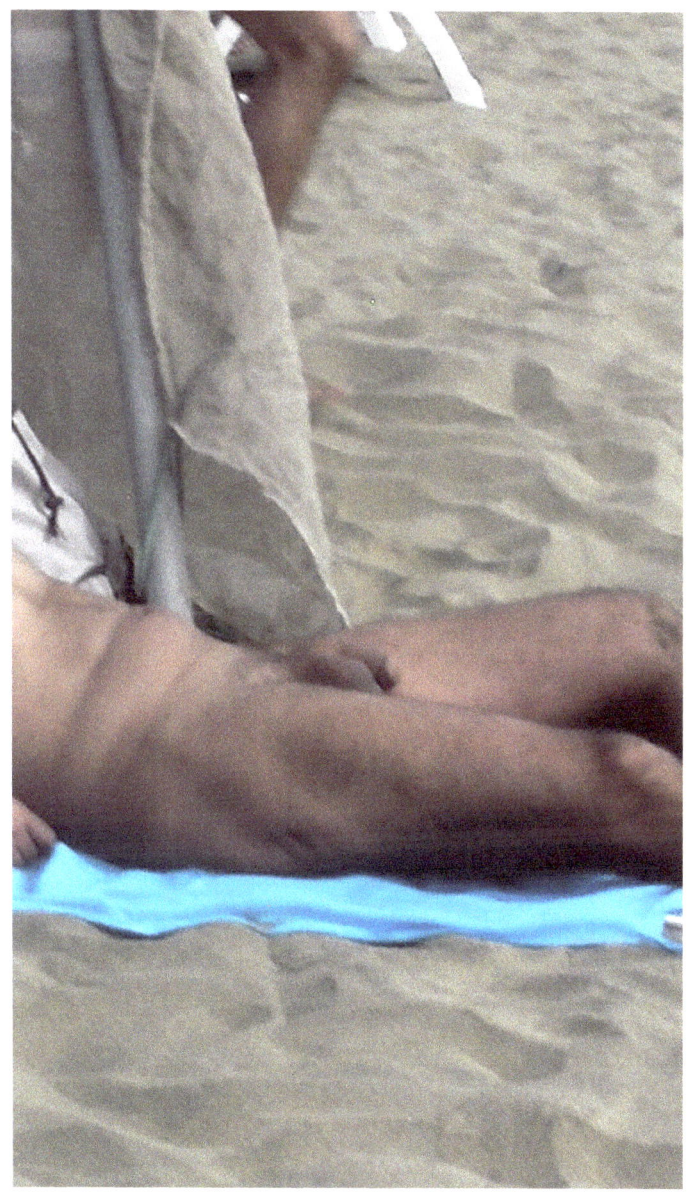

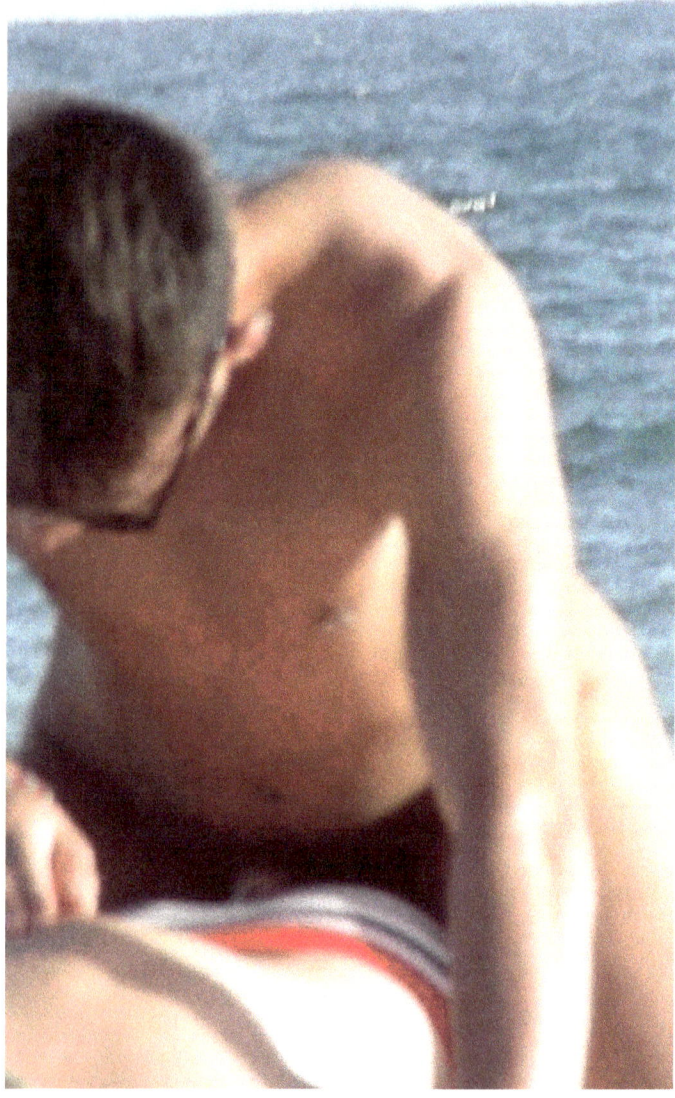

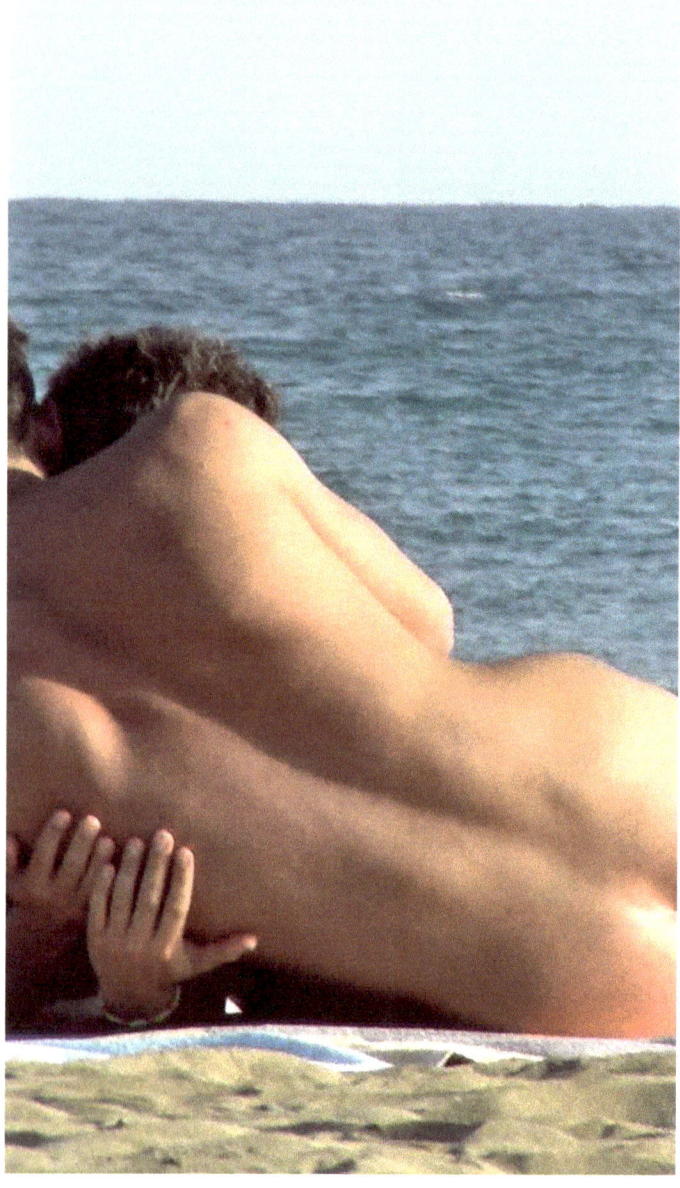

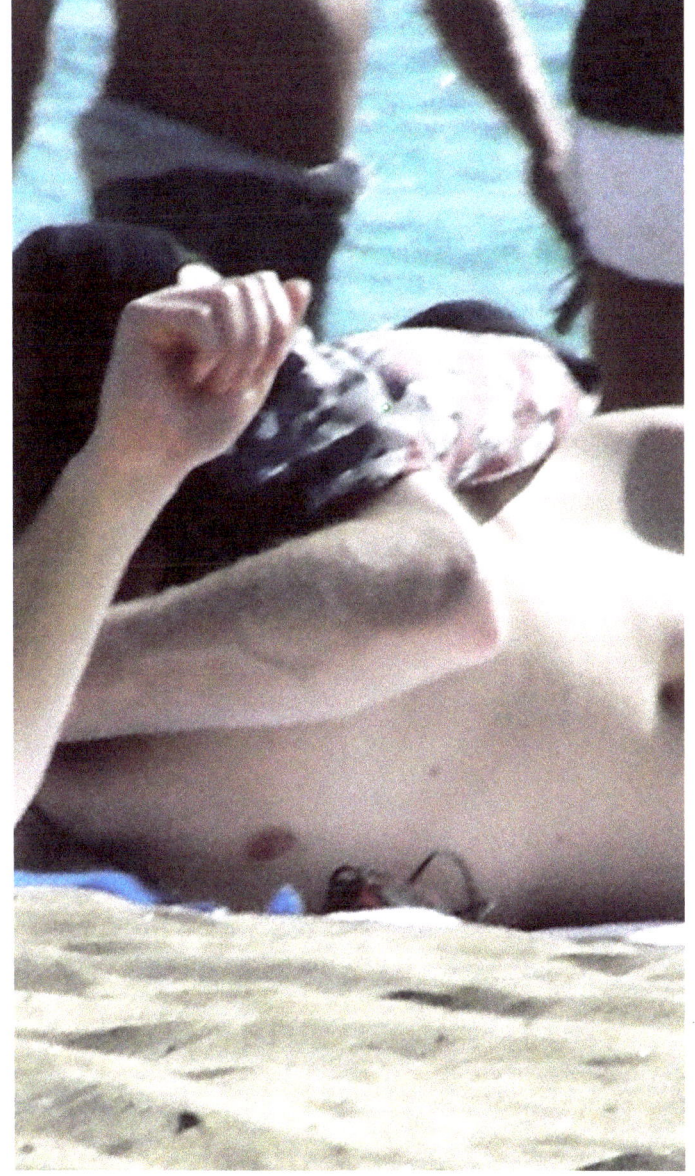

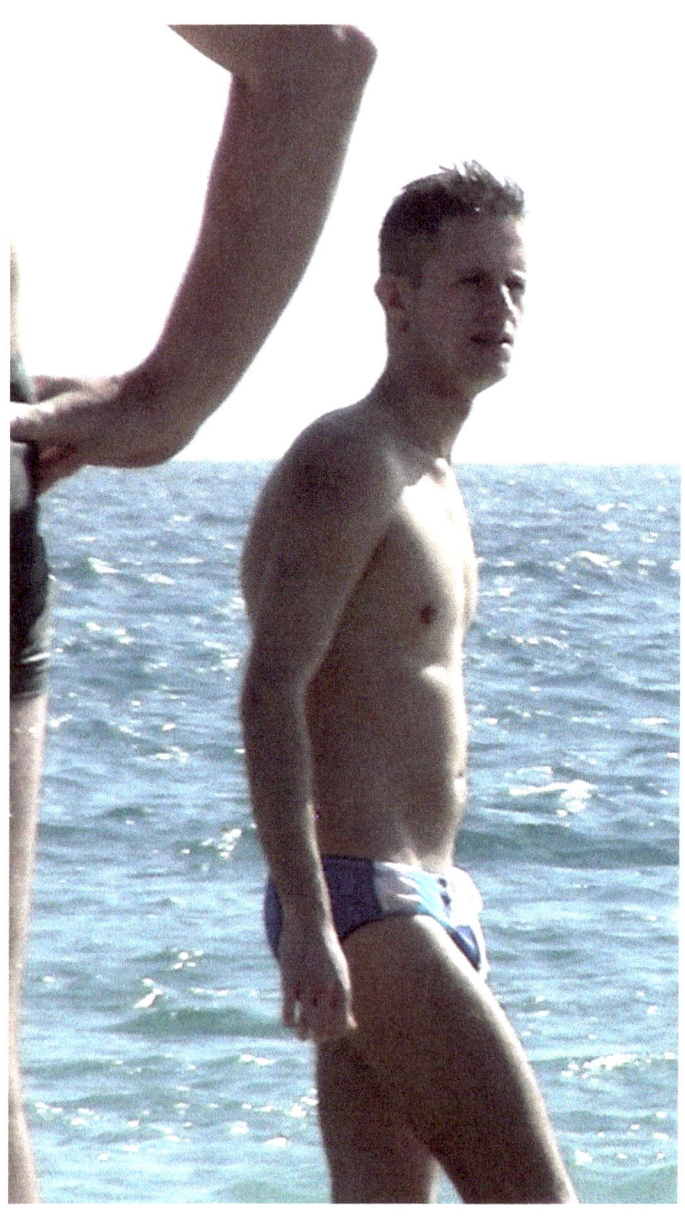

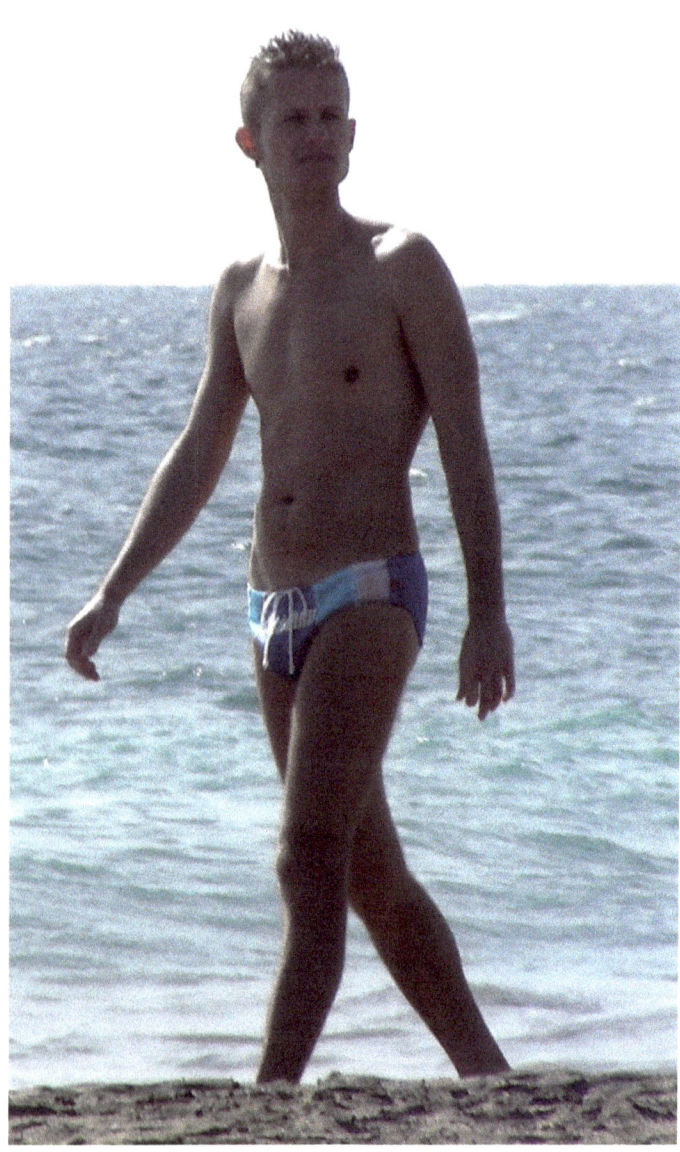

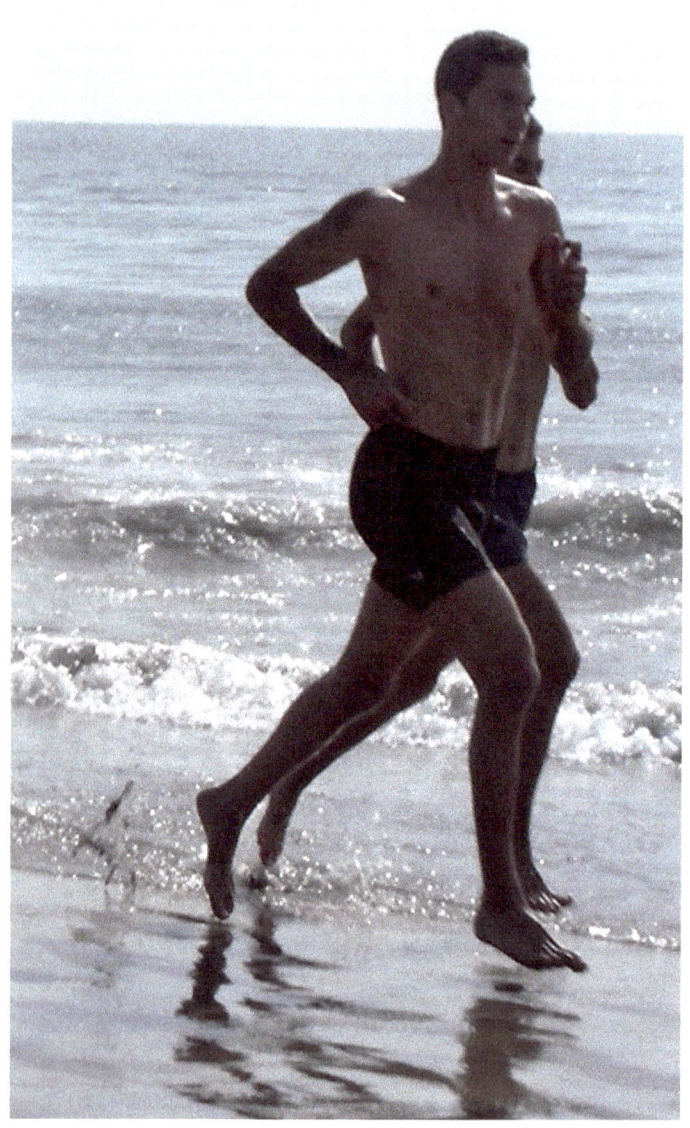

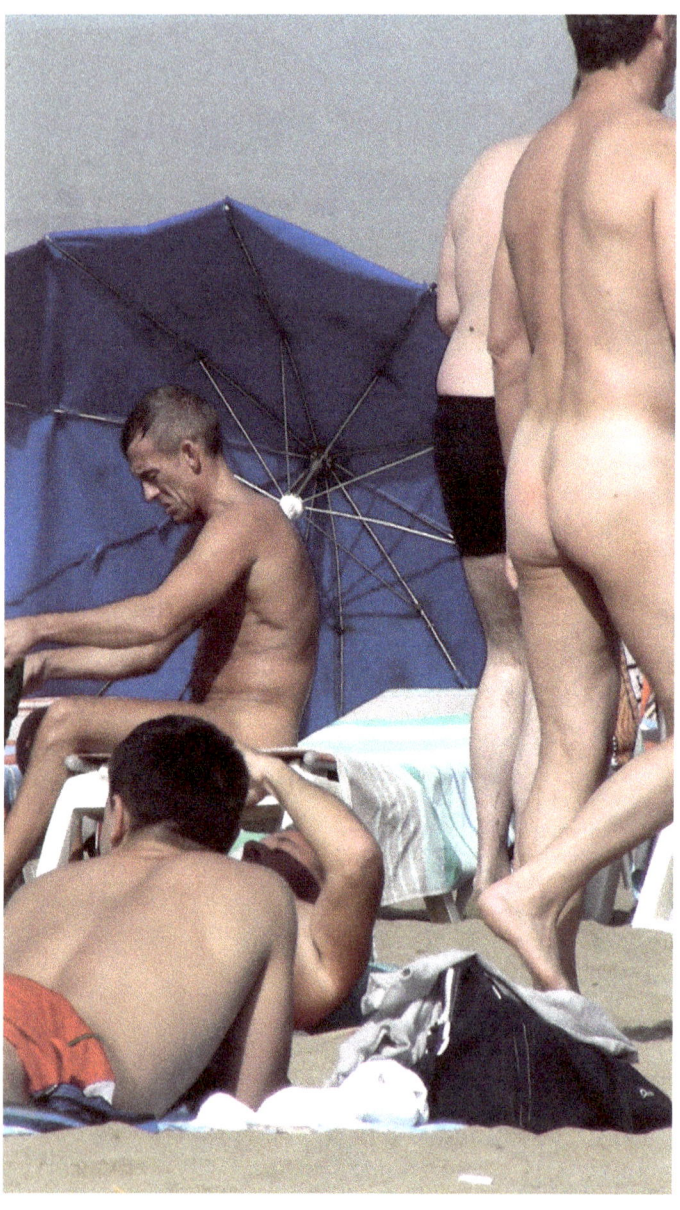

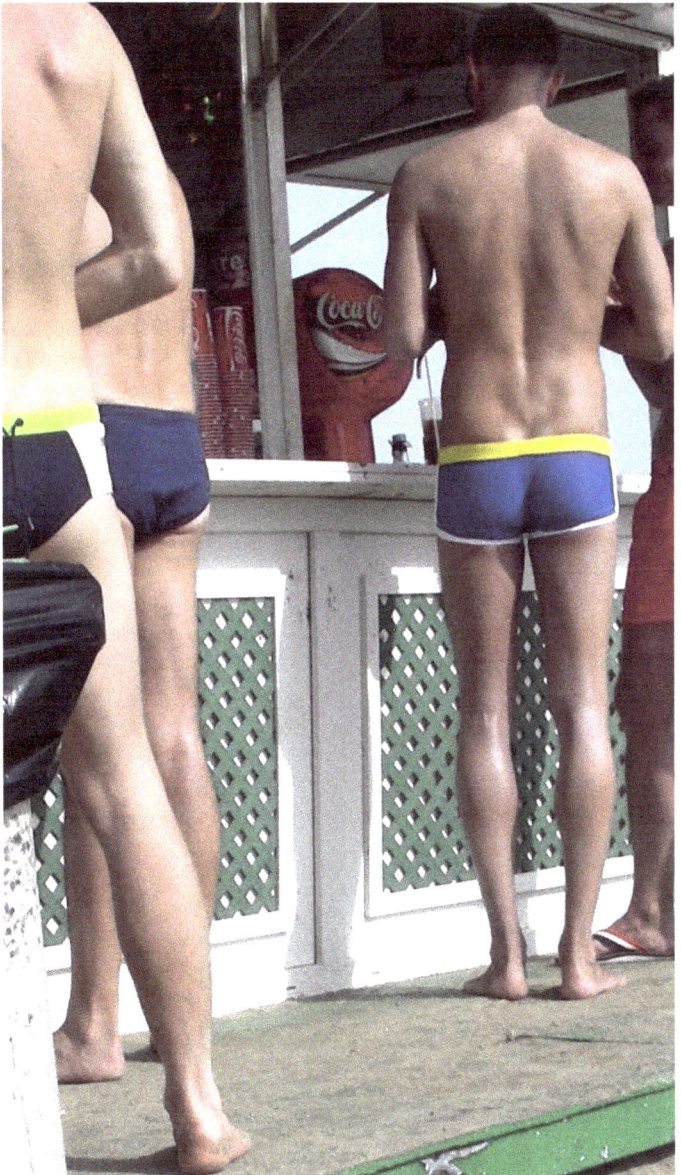

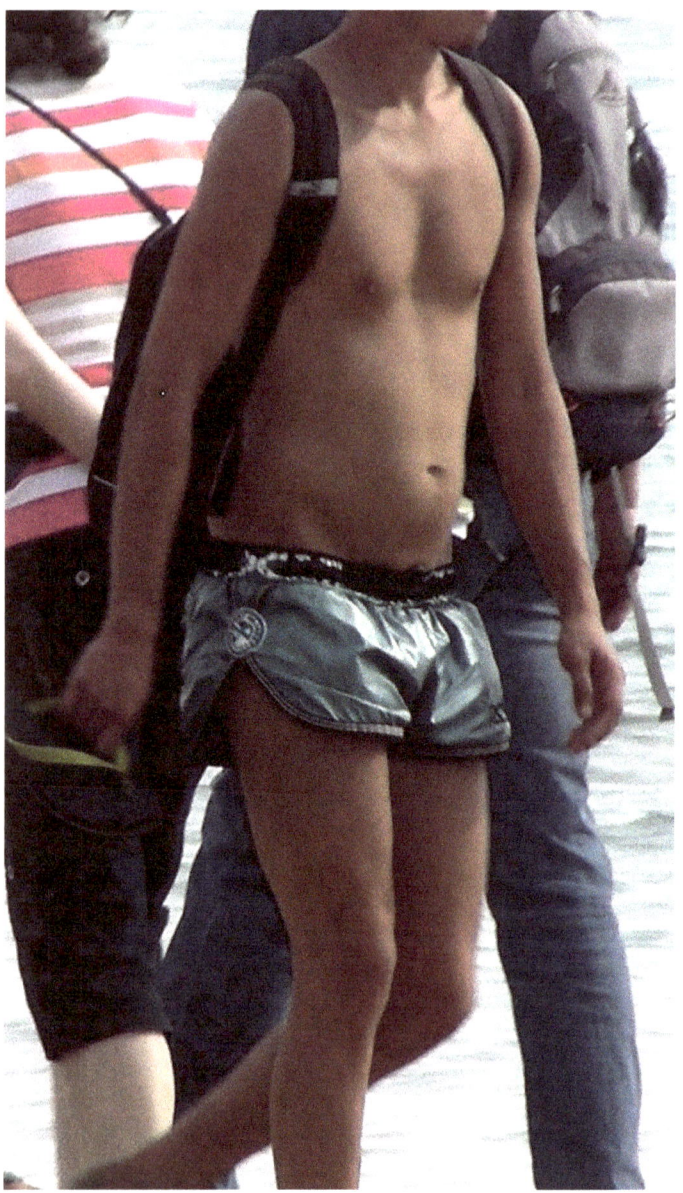

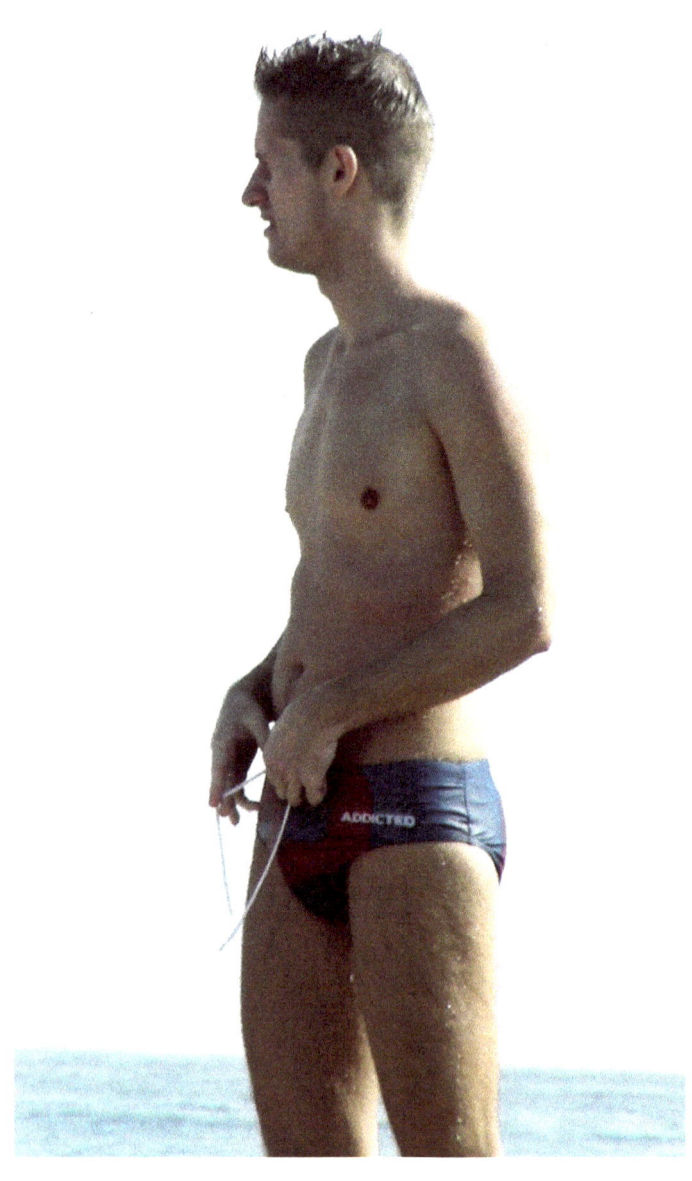

CPSIA information can be obtained
at www.ICGtesting.com
Printed in the USA
BVHW020349300719
554530BV00043B/1576/P

9 780464 069096